ORDER FORM FOR
COMPLETE REPORT OF NATIONAL ASSESSMENT
OF STUDENTS' GLOBAL UNDERSTANDING

Publications Dept.
Council on Learning
271 North Avenue
New Rochelle, N.Y. 10801

Please send me the complete ETS study of college students' knowledge and beliefs about global topics. The full report includes twelve chapters, complete data, questionnaires and all responses, several appendices and bibliography. I enclose $10.95 for postage paid delivery. (For "bill me" orders add $1 for billing and handling.)

_____
name

_____
organization

_____
address

Council on Learning

WHAT COLLEGE STUDENTS KNOW AND BELIEVE ABOUT THEIR WORLD

by

Thomas S. Barrows, Stephen F. Klein, and John L.D. Clark

Educational Testing Service

**This synopsis was written by
Nathaniel Hartshorne
Director, Program Publications
Educational Testing Service**

Change Magazine Press

March 1981

This book is a synopsis of a complete technical report by the Educational Testing Service entitled *College Students' Knowledge and Beliefs: A Survey of Global Understanding* (the full report may be ordered from Change Magazine Press, $10.95 postpaid with prepayment). This volume and several companion publications result from the Education and the World View project of the Council on Learning. Funding for the survey of students' global understanding was provided to ETS by the U.S. Department of Education, with support of the National Endowment for the Humanities. Major funding for the Council's project was provided by the National Endowment for the Humanities and the Exxon Education Foundation.

Contents

Education and the
World View

The Council on Learning established its Education and the World View program in an effort to encourage the nation's colleges and universities to widen the international components in their undergraduate curriculum. The Council sponsors this public program because a more consonant reflection of current world realities in education lies in the best interests of the nation as well as its citizens. This program has been funded by the National Endowment for the Humanities, the United States Department of Education, the Exxon Education Foundation, and the Joyce Mertz-Gilmore Foundation. The various activities under this endeavor are guided by a national task force of 50 leaders in academic, public, and business life. For further information about this project, write to the Council on Learning, 271 North Avenue, New Rochelle, N.Y. 10801.

Foreword

It is difficult to quarrel with facts. This volume, a sharply condensed version of a much larger and fascinating report on the first national test of American collegians about their understanding and beliefs about the larger world, destroys a few myths and begs as many new questions.

No massive test such as this one, containing as it does hundreds of thousands of bits of information, can be easily summarized, let alone quickly comprehended. Suffice it to say that while this national test of students' global understanding proved considerably challenging and intellectually demanding, there is nonetheless sufficient evidence to suggest that this nation is still poorly equipped in terms of its ability to deal with its innumerable global obligations with an adequate public understanding in place. The three thousand college students tested here will be America's leaders at the entry of the twenty-first century. One wonders whether we shall learn our lessons in time that the education of our citizenry must keep apace of the changing circumstances of national existence.

What shows through here is the continued failure of our colleges and universities to effectively temper the usual disciplinary tunnel visions to accommodate a transcendent body of knowledge which fits only poorly the increasing narrowness of scholarly pursuit. The matter can obviously not be left to the disciplines and academic departments alone. Nor can a nation now so irrevocably immersed in global complexities endure for long the fashionable academic obsession with microknowledge refined to fit on the point of a needle. The indictment of that pursuit is here for all to see.

This summary is only a surface indication of the far greater data contained in the full report of this 1980 national test. Those seeking a detailed reading of what college students understand about their world can order the full report by the special form bound into the front of this volume.

George W. Bonham
Council on Learning

2

ETS Project Staff

Sheila M. Ager
Associate Examiner

Thomas S. Barrows
Project Director
Research Scientist

Mary F. Bennett
Research Assistant

Henry I. Braun
Research Scientist

John L. D. Clark
Senior Examiner

Lois D. Harris
Administrative Secretary

Bruce A. Kaplan
Research Data Analyst

Stephen F. Klein
Senior Examiner

Assessment Committee

Robert F. Dernberger
Professor of Economics
University of Michigan

A. David Hill
Professor of Geography
University of Colorado

William J. McGuire
Professor of Psychology
Yale University

William H. McNeill
Robert A. Milliken Distinguished Service Professor of History
University of Chicago

Richard C. Snyder
Director Emeritus, Mershon Center
The Ohio State University

Judith V. Torney-Purta
Professor of Psychology
University of Illinois at Chicago Circle

G. Richard Tucker
Director
Center for Applied Linguistics

Immanuel Wallerstein
Professor of Sociology
State University of New York at Binghamton

I. Introduction

Students graduating from American colleges today generally have acquired some knowledge of the humanities and the social or physical sciences. Whether or not they have at the same time acquired any adequate knowledge of the outside world is not known. How much does the average college senior know and understand about international affairs? How much do two or four years of higher education contribute to a student's sophistication about the world and its enormously complex problems?

These and similar questions have been the central concern of Education and the World View, a two-year project sponsored by the Council on Learning, a nonprofit organization that sponsors research and projects in the area of public policy issues. The Council launched Education and the World View in 1978 to focus public attention on the need to strengthen the international component of the American college curriculum and to stimulate debate on how best to educate young Americans for life in a competitive and shrinking world.

One of the project's major tasks has been to take a scientific sampling of what college students do know about their world. Thus, in 1979, the Council on Learning contracted with Educational Testing Service (ETS) in Princeton, New Jersey, to conduct a nationwide survey of freshmen and seniors in four-year colleges and students in two-year institutions to determine their understanding of the world and world issues. The survey, which was funded by the Office (now the Department) of Education and supported by the National Endowment for the Humanities, was based on a sample of about 3,000 undergraduates at 185 institutions. The survey was conducted in the winter and early spring of 1980.

The survey measures included an ambitious test of global understanding and three questionnaires—on students' backgrounds and interests, their foreign language backgrounds and proficiency, and their attitudes toward foreign nations and world issues.

A Glance at the Outcome

The performance of these students on the test revealed a considerable lack of knowledge of topics the test developers felt were important. The average score for seniors was 50.5 (out of 101 questions); for freshmen, 41.9; and for two-year students, 40.5

All three groups did well on questions concerned with population, physical geography, and arts and culture. Their weakest performance was on questions having to do with energy and religion. Significantly, many students were uninformed about issues that have been widely reported and discussed in the news media. For example, almost half the seniors in the

Which of the following lists is composed entirely of members of OPEC (Organization of Petroleum Exporting Countries)?

(1) Iran, Iraq, Kuwait, Egypt

(2) Great Britain, Norway, Mexico, United Arab Emirates

(3) Syria, Lebanon, Libya, Ethiopia

*(4) Venezuela, Indonesia, Nigeria, Saudi Arabia

* Correct answer

This question stumped 65 percent of the seniors.

sample were unaware of the impact caused by the increase in the world's consumption of oil since the 1960s. More than half the freshmen, for example, thought that OPEC is an exclusively all-Middle East organization that also includes Egypt.

Even those students who were above-average scorers had serious misconceptions about many key world issues and facts. Among them were these:

- The causes of inadequate nutrition;
- The United States' record on signing human rights treaties adopted by the United Nations and the major accomplishment of the Helsinki Accords;
- The comparative world membership of Islam and Christianity and the countries in which Islam predominates or has a significant minority;
- The difficulties connected with either national self-sufficiency or dependency in a world of interdependent nations;

Since the Second World War, the gap in per capita income between the world's richest and poorest countries has

*(1) widened

(2) remained about the same

(3) narrowed slightly

(4) narrowed substantially

Students scored well on this question.

- The historical origins of the Western sovereign territorial state and the modern state system and the emergence of nationalist movements as significant political forces in European history;
- The reasons for the lack of substantial progress toward world peace during the twentieth century.

Almost 90 percent of the seniors reported in the language questionnaire that they had learned or studied a foreign language. Relatively few of these respondents, however, felt that they could put their language education to much use. Although almost half the seniors said they could "quite easily" introduce themselves in social situations and use appropriate greetings and farewells in the language they had studied, only one-third could as easily order a simple meal in a restaurant or ask for directions on the street. Almost all (98 percent) of the seniors in the sample felt that they could not easily understand a foreign movie without reading subtitles.

There was *no* significant correlation between students' proficiency in foreign languages and their performance on the test of global understanding.

The Full ETS Report
The development and content of the questions in the test and the questionnaires, the results of the survey, and an interpretation of the results are all discussed in the pages that follow. The full ETS survey report, *College Students' Knowledge and Beliefs: A Survey of Global Understanding*, presents a far more detailed discussion of the survey, with appendices containing all the survey materials and response data.

In addition to this survey report, ETS and the Council on Learning have designed a series of curriculum workshops and self-evaluation kits for institutions that are interested in reviewing, broadening, or establishing international curriculum programs.

II. The Survey

The notion of *global understanding*—of being aware of nations beyond one's borders and of the issues that involve those nations and one's own—is a relatively modern one. Moreover, it is not well understood; little has been done to define the concept. When the ETS staff of research scientists and test development specialists began to design the Education and World View survey, they had to proceed on the assumption that global understanding is more than a knowledge (or cognitive) concept; that it also involves feelings (affect). The survey, therefore, would have to touch on students' attitudes and interests as well as knowledge and abilities, and to measure both.

The researchers were also interested in discovering what skills or activities contribute to global understanding. For example, what is the relationship, if any, between interest or proficiency in foreign languages and an understanding of the world or a foreign culture? Questionnaires would have to be developed to find out how closely language skills and other aspects of students' backgrounds were associated with their knowledge of the world.

The Knowledge Test
One of the more difficult tasks the project staff grappled with in designing the survey instruments was to decide on an approach to take in constructing the knowledge test. Without a clear definition of global understanding, how does one decide what specific knowledge it consists of? Does global knowledge mean an understanding of the kind of content taught in traditional college courses in international relations and area studies? Or does it mean a grasp of global issues, such as human rights or world government, that transcend particular nations and regions?

In deciding these and other questions, the project team sought the counsel of an assessment committee of distinguished scholars, each of whom possessed knowledge both of a major area of the world and of a relevant academic discipline. The scholars on this committee were clearly inclined toward adopting an issues approach for the knowledge test because of the implicitly global scope and the multiple dimensions that characterize many issues. Such an approach would enable the survey team to get at students' knowledge of an issue in its present context as well as its historical roots.

As work on the test progressed, members of the world studies faculty at Eisenhower College (now the Eisenhower Campus of the Rochester Institute of Technology) in Seneca Falls, New York, further helped define issues for the committee, and experts in various disciplines at numerous colleges and universities helped the ETS test specialists shape the final test instrument.

Although their questions focused on issues, the writers took care to build into each one disciplinary elements of the issue that seemed relevant. A question on world oil reserves, for example, might call for knowledge of geology, politics, and geography as well as economics. The survey staff and the committee agreed that the knowledge test should not assess formal knowledge of a discipline but rather the kind of awareness of a discipline one has from studying related courses in college or reading newspapers and magazines.

The final version of the knowledge test consisted of 101 questions (96 of which were written for this test and five taken from a test for high school students developed and administered by ETS several years ago). The questions clustered around 13 topics: environment, food, health, population, international monetary and trade arrangements, energy, race and ethnicity, human rights, war and armaments, arts and culture, religious issues, relations among states, and distribution of natural characteristics (physical geography). The test stressed the themes of interdependence among nations, the problems of developing nations, and such historical transformations that the committee members and the ETS staff felt to be important to an understanding of the modern world.

Measuring Attitudes
Knowing is only one side of understanding. To explore the other side of students' understanding of the world meant uncovering their *attitudes* toward the world's nations, peoples, and issues.

The project staff approached this task from several different directions. One series of questions was designed to determine how the students perceive world issues. They were asked to rate a number of world problems, such as environmental pollution, depletion of natural resources, and inflation, on several descriptive scales (*This problem is important/This problem is unimportant; The American government can do a lot to solve this problem/The American government can do very little to solve this problem; This problem is [is not] interesting to learn about, etc.*).

An opinion survey asked the students to indicate the extent of their agreement with each of 32 statements on such topics as chauvinism (*Patriotism and loyalty are the first and most important requirements of a good citizen*), world government (*We should have a World Government with the power to make laws that would be binding to all its member nations*), and war (*War is a satisfactory way to solve international problems*).

A self-report, a type of measure used primarily in personality assessment, was administered to get at students' perceptions of themselves. They were asked to reply true or false to descriptive statements about themselves such as *I make an effort to meet people from other countries* and *I am most comfortable with people from my own culture.*

The Foreign Language Component
Although it is generally accepted by the foreign language teaching profession that the study of a foreign language is of considerable value in developing knowledge of and sensitivity to other countries and cultures, there is little or no research data to support such an assumption. The global understanding survey, therefore, offered an excellent opportunity to investigate the relationships between proficiency, interest, and background in languages and global understanding.

Data collection instruments for this portion of the survey were needed to obtain three different types of information:

● The foreign language background of respondents, including foreign language study at the elementary, secondary, and college levels as well as language contacts outside the academic setting;

- Personal interest in and motivation for learning foreign languages;
- Actual proficiency in a modern language—that is, the ability to use the language in each of a variety of real-life situations that might be encountered outside the classroom.

The language background section contained 17 questions on such subjects as the native language of the respondent and members of his/her family, travel to a foreign country (including summer-abroad or year-abroad programs), service in the Peace Corps and other programs, and average grades in foreign language courses.

To measure motivation and interest in foreign languages, the ETS staff designed an attitude measure that asked students to indicate their agreement with 15 statements about foreign languages. Some examples:

- I enjoy meeting people who speak other languages;
- It is important for Americans to learn foreign languages;
- Learning a foreign language is unnecessary because English is spoken almost everywhere;
- If I had to stay for an extended period of time in a country whose language I did not know at all, I would make an effort to learn that language even though I could get along in that country by using English.

Gathering data on the first two types of information was relatively easy since there were instruments that could be adapted for the purpose. Obtaining information on students' language proficiency, however, proved far more difficult. For one reason, the tests that might have been used to measure such skills were limited to the most widely taught languages and could not begin to cover all the languages that such a large sample of students could be expected to speak. Moreover, such tests were not appropriate for assessing understanding of the speech one hears on radio and television programs, in telephone conversations, PA system announcements, and other real-life situations the ETS staff were interested in measuring. For these reasons as well as the prohibitive cost of administering language tests to 3,000 students across the country, it was decided to ask the students to describe their own proficiency in foreign languages. Since the survey materials were to be completed anonymously and did not count toward course grades, there was no danger of students overestimating or in any other way distorting the information about their language competency.

The language questionnaire consisted of 33 statements about speaking, listening to, and reading foreign languages. The statements concerned skills ranging from naming the days of the week or understanding very simple questions like "What is your name?" to being able to describe the role played by Congress in the U.S. government, understanding a native speaker who is talking quickly and colloquially, or reading highly technical information. To each of these "can do" skills statements, the students were asked to rate their proficiency level as "Quite Easily," "With Some Difficulty," or "With Great Difficulty or Not at All."

The project staff validated these self-assessment statements by presurvey tests in which students' responses to the "can do" statements were compared with their scores on the Modern Language Association's tests of reading and listening as well as their performance in face-to-face language-proficiency interviews. The results of this pretesting showed a sufficiently positive relationship between what the students indicated they could do and what the test scores and interviews revealed.

Backgrounds and Interests
To determine if any particular events or situations in the students' lives, such as experiences at home, at school or elsewhere, family traditions and ties, and interests (other than in foreign languages) were associated with world understanding, the ETS staff developed an extensive questionnaire on the students' backgrounds and interests. Data were collected

on place of birth of students and their parents, political preference of parents, and socioeconomic status. Since it seemed likely that educational experiences in and out of school could contribute importantly to an interest in other nations and cultures, items were included on subjects studied in high school and college as well as grades and scores received on college admissions tests.

The ways in which students acquire information about current events and their interest or lack of interest in those events could influence the development of global understanding. The survey therefore asked about the various news media and the number of hours spent reading, watching, or listening. Three items designed to measure students' interest in world problems were built into this section. Rather than asking students simply to rate a series of problems (important/unimportant, avoidable/unavoidable, etc.), these questions asked them to rank them from 1 to 10 in the order of their felt importance and interest. The third item consisted of a list of 16 fictitious headlines. The students were asked to indicate which of the articles they would read if they had time to read only four. Categories of the articles, as indicated by the headlines, were international news, national news, science and technology news, and sports news.

The Survey and the Sample
The survey was carried out in February and early March of 1980. The knowledge test and background, language, and attitude questionnaires were sent to 197 colleges, universities, and two-year institutions in the Northeast, Midwest, Southeast, and Southwest. One hundred eighty-eight institutions administered and returned materials to ETS; booklets from one institution were lost in the mail.

The sample consisted of approximately 1,000 freshmen, 1,000 seniors, and 1,000 students from two-year colleges, whose average age was 22. The three groups were predominantly female. "White or Caucasian" students constituted the majority of all groups, "Black or Afro-American" the largest minority. Significant numbers of seniors (3.5 percent) and two-year students (3.1 percent) identified with various ethnic backgrounds.

III.   The Results

The Knowledge Test

The maximum score on the knowledge test was 101. The average score for freshmen was 41.9, for seniors, 50.5, and for two-year students, 40.5. Scores ranged from 0 to 84.

Results of the knowledge test indicated that the three student populations were similar to each other in the kind of things they know and don't know about the world's peoples, cultures, and issues. All three groups scored well on issues of health, distribution of natural characteristics (physical geography), arts and culture, and population. They scored poorly on questions having to do with energy, relations among states, and religion.

Considering the performance of these students from a disciplinary point of view, all three groups performed more strongly on the questions having to do with social sciences than they did on questions concerned with the humanities. Items on issues requiring some knowledge of their historical context proved to be stumbling blocks for more of the sample than any other single discipline. (This may help explain why history majors did comparatively well on the test, achieving an average of 59.30. Students majoring in social sciences scored above the average [52.77], but were outperformed by engineering and mathematics majors. Surprisingly, foreign language majors were slightly below the average [50.22]. Lowest of all groups were education majors, whose scores averaged 39.83.)

It seems likely that knowledge gained from careful and regular newspaper reading might have accounted for the seniors' strong performance on some of the questions. For example, 48 percent and 54 percent of the senior population chose the correct answers to these two questions:

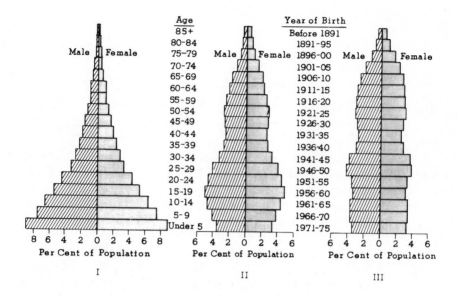

The pyramids above represent the populations of Sweden, Mexico, and the United States in 1975. Which of the following correctly matches each pyramid with the country whose population it represents?

	I	II	III
(1)*	Mexico	United States	Sweden
(2)	United States	Mexico	Sweden
(3)	Mexico	Sweden	United States
(4)	Sweden	United States	Mexico

Which of the following aspects of Western education has had the most profound influence on revolutionary leaders of the Third World who were educated in the West?

(1) Humanities
(2) Physical and biological sciences
(3) Industrial technology
(4) *Social and political theories

Almost 70 percent of the seniors knew the answer to this question about the Soviet view of the United States:

In its official interpretations of United States foreign policy, Soviet doctrine tends to emphasize which of the following arguments?

(1) The United States is a democracy; consequently, its foreign policy is driven by the aggressive aims of the masses.
(2) *The United States is a state under the control of monopoly capitalists, and as such, it is an imperialist power.
(3) The United States is a disguised dictatorship; therefore its foreign policy reflects the territorial ambitions of its military leaders.
(4) Internal divisions weaken the United States; hence, it is a paper tiger and can safely be defied.

The assessment committee and the ETS staff were interested in discovering what the students did *not* know as well as what they knew about the world. A serious effort was made, therefore, to construct knowledge questions with incorrect answer choices that would reveal misconceptions among students. Of the 101 questions on the test, 24 drew incorrect response choices from the more able students (those whose scores on the test were higher than the average score for their group). These questions are shown on pages 18-26. The percentage of students choosing particular responses is shown under each question. The correct answer is asterisked. Options chosen by more able students are indicated by underlining of percentages.

Of the 24 questions shown here, six (1, 10, 13, 14, 16, and 24) attracted able students in all three groups to the same incorrect answers. All these are social science questions concerned with recent and current global affairs. More than 40 percent of the more able students in all three groups chose the first answer choice for question 1. This answer showed the annual world consumption of fossil fuels to be more than 10 billion tons before the year 1000. A greater proportion of seniors than any of the other two groups chose the wrong answer to five of these six questions (10, 13, 14, 16, and 24). Of all the 24 questions shown here, number 13 proved to be the one that drew the largest proportion of able students to one incorrect answer—that the global problem of inadequate nutrition is a matter of insufficient production rather than inequitable distribution.

The information sampled by question 24 (about the distribution of the world's diseases) is more likely to be acquired in academic courses than through the news media, and it is possible that many of the students in this sample did not have access to such courses. On the other hand, the topics covered by questions 1, 10, 14, and 16—fossil fuel consumption, world population trends, the difficulties of economic development in predominantly agricultural countries, and the Helsinki Accords—have received extensive news coverage. Despite the fact that the subject matter of these four questions is fairly general information to which all students would have access, approximately 2 out of 5 students in the sample had an unrealistic view of past and future fossil use; 1 out of 3 thought that world population growth is accelerating; 1 out of 5 considered the mechanization of agriculture to be the only avenue to economic development in predominantly agricultural countries; and more than 1 out of 4 thought that the Helsinki Accords had established a court where human rights complaints could be heard.

Responses to some of the other questions were more divergent. In question 3, for example, while 7 percent of the seniors thought that the membership of OPEC included Syria, Lebanon, and Ethiopia as well as Libya, more than half the freshmen and nearly half the two-year students thought that OPEC is an all-Middle East organization that includes Egypt. Despite the prominence given to the world energy situation since 1973, only 2 out of 5 seniors and roughly 1 out of 3 freshmen and two-year college students were aware of the impact of the total world increase in the use of oil since the early 1960s.

Questions on the history and precepts of the world's major religions tripped up large numbers of these students. On three of the questions (6, 7, and 9), the percentage answering correctly ranged as low as 9 to 14 percent. Performance on the other two (5 and 8) ranged no higher than 29 to 34 percent. Over half the freshman and two-year groups were unaware of the origins of the World Zionist Organization. These are humanities items and it is quite possible that the students in the sample had had less exposure to this kind of subject matter than to social science topics. The subjects have, however, been covered extensively by the news media in stories and editorials about the resurgence of Islam, events in Iran, and the Soviet invasion of Afghanistan.

Questions based on history caused trouble. Large numbers of seniors, freshmen, and two-year students did not know the answer to question 12—that people of Mexican descent were already living in areas conquered or annexed by the United States in the mid-nineteenth century. Students were also weak in their knowledge of the historical origins of the Western territorial state (question 19). And only 23 percent of the total student population correctly answered question 23 about the efforts to build world peace in the twentieth century. On the history item about the establishment of the Soviet Union shown below, which was taken from a 1974 ETS survey of high school seniors, 61 percent of the college seniors did not know that the republics of that nation were formed on the basis of ethnic nationalities.

The republics of the Soviet Union were formed primarily on the basis of

(1)*   the ethnic groups or nationalities of the people.
(2)   natural geographic boundaries.
(3)   the political orientation of the people.
(4)   agricultural and climatic zones.

Percentage of Students Selecting Responses[1]

	12th Grade	Freshmen	Seniors	2-Year
(1)*	23	25	36	24
(2)	26	25	21	23
(3)	37	33	26	35
(4)	14	13	14	14

[1]Freshmen, seniors, and students at 2-year colleges are represented by samples of approximately 1,000 each. Twelfth-grade students are represented by samples of 550 to 600 each.

Some Sample Questions

(responses in percent)

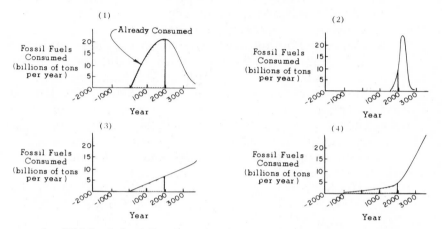

1. Which of the following curves best represents the estimates of experts about the pattern of the world's past and possible future consumption of fossil fuels such as petroleum, natural gas, and coal?

	(1)	(2)*	(3)	(4)
Seniors	41.5	28.2	16.7	9.8
Freshmen	43.8	21.3	17.0	13.0
Two-Year	43.6	16.7	17.8	14.6

2. President Carter was primarily concerned about which of the following when he urged all nations to defer nuclear fuel reprocessing and the development of the breeder reactor?

    (1) The possibility of nuclear weapons proliferation
    (2) The occurrence of a catastrophic accident
    (3) The emergence of a uranium cartel
    (4) The distortion of economic development priorities

	(1)*	(2)	(3)	(4)
Seniors	43.5	37.6	5.5	11.6
Freshmen	36.0	40.0	6.3	13.1
Two-Year	44.3	35.2	5.3	12.0

3. Which of the following lists is composed entirely of members of OPEC (Organization of Petroleum Exporting Countries)?

    (1) Iran, Iraq, Kuwait, Egypt

(2) Great Britain, Norway, Mexico, United Arab Emirates
(3) Syria, Lebanon, Libya, Ethiopia
(4) Venezuela, Indonesia, Nigeria, Saudi Arabia

	(1)	(2)	(3)	(4)*
Seniors	57.5	2.1	6.7	29.1
Freshmen	56.2	7.3	8.5	21.1
Two-Year	48.7	8.1	7.9	27.9

4. Which of the following helps to explain the ability of OPEC (Organization of Petroleum Exporting Countries) to raise oil prices since 1973?

   (1) OPEC countries have become controlled uniformly by groups hostile to capitalism and the West.
   (2) OPEC countries have experienced a significant growth in their military strength.
   (3) There has been a large increase in total world industrial production and transport since the early 1960s.
   (4) The value of the dollar has declined.

	(1)	(2)	(3)*	(4)
Seniors	22.0	8.4	40.2	23.8
Freshmen	16.0	12.7	32.9	30.7
Two-Year	14.4	13.4	31.1	32.4

5. Which grouping of the religions below presents them in descending size of estimated world membership?

   (1) Christianity, Buddhism, Islam, Hinduism, Judaism
   (2) Islam, Christianity, Hinduism, Buddhism, Judaism
   (3) Hinduism, Islam, Christianity, Judaism, Buddhism
   (4) Christianity, Islam, Hinduism, Buddhism, Judaism

	(1)	(2)	(3)	(4)*
Seniors	16.2	23.9	24.7	31.8
Freshmen	20.9	21.8	17.2	36.0
Two-Year	28.2	15.9	18.8	31.1

6. Each religion below is correctly matched with countries in *each* of which it either predominates or has a significant minority following EXCEPT

   (1) Christianity...Greece, Lebanon, the Philippines, Ethiopia
   (2) Islam...Saudia Arabia, the Soviet Union, Indonesia, Nigeria
   (3) Buddhism....Japan, Thailand, Vietnam, Sri Lanka (Ceylon)
   (4) Hinduism...India, Pakistan, Afghanistan, Kampuchea (Cambodia)

	(1)	(2)	(3)	(4)*
Seniors	31.9	42.0	7.2	13.0
Freshmen	29.2	39.8	13.2	12.5
Two-Year	33.4	31.1	14.3	11.7

7. The World Zionist Organization, which sought the creation of a Jewish state, was founded in response to

   (1) the anti-Semitism that surrounded the Dreyfus case at the end of the nineteenth century.
   (2) the British government's 1917 declaration in support of the concept of a Jewish national homeland.
   (3) Stalin's anti-Semitic purges in the 1930s.
   (4) Nazi persecution of the Jews.

	(1)*	(2)	(3)	(4)
Seniors	11.0	18.8	12.5	50.0
Freshmen	10.2	16.9	13.6	51.3
Two-Year	9.7	12.3	11.1	55.9

8. One of Buddhism's most basic teachings is that

   (1) one can be saved from sin if one learns to suppress anger and fear.
   (2) human life is a cycle of suffering caused by individual desires.
   (3) everyone who wishes to be saved from sin must become a monk or a nun.
   (4) the Buddha was the final divinely inspired prophet sent to the human race.

	(1)	(2)*	(3)	(4)
Seniors	11.6	39.5	9.5	34.4
Freshmen	9.6	29.8	11.3	42.9
Two-Year	12.1	29.2	9.7	40.1

9. Which of the following is shared by Christianity, Judaism, Islam, Buddhism, and Hinduism?

   (1) The concept of a messiah
   (2) A general tendency to proselytize
   (3) A tradition of mysticism
   (4) Insistence on personal identification with a single religion

	(1)	(2)	(3)*	(4)
Seniors	35.1	5.4	13.8	42.6
Freshmen	36.6	6.1	11.0	41.5
Two-Year	35.9	6.2	9.3	43.0

10. Which of the following statements describes the trend in world population growth as of 1980?

   (1) It is accelerating and total population is expected to triple by the year 2000.
   (2) It is accelerating and total population is expected to double by the year 2000.
   (3) It has begun to decelerate, but total population is still expected to increase substantially by the year 2000.
   (4) It has started to decelerate, and therefore total population is expected to decline by the year 2000.

	(1)	(2)	(3)*	(4)
Seniors	6.6	36.8	52.6	3.1
Freshmen	9.9	33.1	48.9	5.1
Two-Year	10.7	33.9	46.1	7.4

11. The largest groups of people living outside their home countries in 1978-1979 were made up of

   (1) political refugees leaving or fleeing their countries.
   (2) foreign workers and their families working and residing in West European countries.
   (3) legal and illegal immigrants to the United States.
   (4) military forces of the United States and the Soviet Union stationed in the territories of allied countries.

	(1)	(2)*	(3)	(4)
Seniors	36.0	10.9	31.1	19.9
Freshmen	31.0	10.2	41.2	15.8
Two-Year	37.1	8.6	43.0	10.7

12. Which of the following is a correct statement about the historical sources of population in North and South America?

   (1) During the mid-eighteenth-century struggle between England and France for dominance in Canada, the French were a minority of the Canadian white population.
   (2) By the beginning of the nineteenth century, all major areas of European settlement on the South American continent were under Spanish domination.
   (3) The first sizable number of people of Mexican descent in the United States were resident in areas conquered or annexed by the United States in the mid-nineteenth century.
   (4) In the massive influx of European immigrants into the United States during the late nineteenth and early twentieth centuries, Northern Europeans predominated over immigrants from Eastern and Southern Europe.

	(1)	(2)	(3)*	(4)
Seniors	8.4	19.7	35.1	30.4
Freshmen	11.1	22.9	25.5	31.3
Two-Year	13.4	21.2	30.3	27.4

13. As a global problem, inadequate nutrition is largely the result of

   (1) large populations living in countries whose production of foodstuffs is insufficient to provide the minimum number of calories required by each person each day.
   (2) world population having outgrown the world's ability to produce enough food to meet each person's daily caloric requirements.
   (3) large populations living in countries in which inequalities of income result in a significant portion of the population being unable to buy the foods produced by others.
   (4) trade controls that prevent food surpluses produced by some countries from being exported to other countries that want to buy them.

	(1)	(2)	(3)*	(4)
Seniors	61.3	10.4	24.3	3.0
Freshmen	51.5	14.4	27.0	4.3
Two-Year	48.7	15.9	28.0	5.5

14. Most countries that have a majority of their populations working in agriculture and earn most of their foreign exchange from agriculture exports are finding economic development difficult because

   (1) there is a declining world market for agricultural products.
   (2) they can only develop through mechanization of agriculture, but this will create large-scale unemployment.
   (3) they are especially vulnerable to both crop failures and world price fluctuations.
   (4) the income of the majority of the population depends upon export earnings.

	(1)	(2)	(3)*	(4)
Seniors	2.5	21.5	65.8	6.9
Freshmen	6.2	19.5	57.9	9.2
Two-Year	7.7	19.6	51.2	12.3

15. In China one-third of the farmland and sixty percent of the rural labor force are devoted to growing rice. The major advantage to China of growing rice is that

   (1) China has surplus farm labor and few alternatives for employment.

(2) the weight, the nutrient, and the market value of rice per unit of land are much higher than those of other basic grain crops.

(3) rice, as the major grain involved in world trade, is principally grown for foreign markets to earn foreign exchange.

(4) the extra labor required for growing rice largely consists of women and children, a fact that makes the cost of growing rice less than that of growing other grains.

	(1)	(2)*	(3)	(4)
Seniors	26.2	30.4	14.4	24.9
Freshmen	19.9	25.6	18.1	31.2
Two-Year	17.4	22.3	25.8	28.4

16. In the area of human rights, the major accomplishment of the Helsinki Accords was the

(1) establishment of a court where human rights complaints can be heard.

(2) acknowledgment of the signatories' right to intercede in the event one of their members violates human rights.

(3) commitment made by the United States to admit as an immigrant any Eastern European who can show that his or her human rights have been violated.

(4) recognition accorded human rights as a legitimate subject of discussion in the East-West debate.

	(1)	(2)	(3)	(4)*
Seniors	27.4	13.9	12.2	28.6
Freshmen	26.1	15.6	19.3	19.8
Two-Year	27.9	14.1	18.0	25.0

17. In the period between 1945 and 1975, the United Nations adopted nearly 20 human rights treaties, such as the Genocide convention. These treaties must be ratified by a certain number of member countries before going into effect. About how many of these treaties did the United States ratify?

(1) Nearly all of them
(2) More than half of them
(3) Fewer than half of them
(4) Almost none of them

	(1)	(2)	(3)*	(4)
Seniors	51.5	29.6	9.3	2.5
Freshmen	40.3	28.9	19.5	4.7
Seniors	38.6	29.9	19.1	4.9

18. Which of the following organizations promulgated the Universal Declaration of Human Rights?

(1) The League of Nations in 1919 following the First World War
(2) The World Council of Churches in 1936 following the outbreak of the Spanish Civil War
(3) The United Nations in 1948 following the Second World War
(4) Amnesty International in 1972 following a terrorist attack at the Olympic Games

	(1)	(2)	(3)*	(4)
Seniors	21.6	5.9	51.6	10.3
Freshmen	21.0	7.9	49.9	10.7
Two-Year	20.5	7.9	46.0	15.2

19. The establishment of the Western sovereign territorial state and the modern state system is usually dated from the

(1) breakup of the Roman Empire in the fifth century.
(2) development of feudalism in the early Middle Ages.
(3) Peace of Westphalia in the mid-seventeenth century, which brought European conflicts fought in the name of religion to an end.
(4) Peace of Versailles in the early twentieth century, which dealt with the aftermath of the breakup of the Russian, German, Austro-Hungarian, and Ottoman empires.

	(1)	(2)	(3)*	(4)
Seniors	13.2	20.5	19.0	37.4
Freshmen	15.3	18.4	18.9	36.2
Two-Year	16.8	21.4	17.6	34.4

20. A very high degree of interdependence is a basic fact of contemporary international life. Which of the following is NOT a significant consequence of interdependence?

(1) Interdependence intermingles domestic with foreign policies.
(2) Interdependence is associated with an increased willingness to renounce war as an instrument of national policy.
(3) Interdependence makes it highly probable that significant events in, or actions by, nation A will have serious effects on nations B, C, D, etc., and vice versa.
(4) Interdependence may make both self-sufficiency and dependency (e.g., reliance on imports of essential raw materials) difficult and costly.

	(1)	(2)*	(3)	(4)
Seniors	15.8	33.2	14.6	28.1
Freshmen	14.6	23.2	24.2	25.1
Two-Year	13.8	28.3	25.2	24.5

21. Unlike trade negotiations in the 1940s, 1950s, and 1960s, the main purpose of the recently completed multilateral trade negotiations was to
    (1) lower tariffs and customs duties.
    (2) establish stable prices for petroleum products.
    (3) reduce nontariff barriers to trade.
    (4) reduce the trade barriers of less developed countries.

	(1)	(2)	(3)*	(4)
Seniors	15.2	28.5	18.0	26.3
Freshmen	16.0	36.3	13.0	25.5
Two-Year	19.4	32.4	13.0	26.2

22. In the North-South talks, representatives of developing countries have demanded all of the following EXCEPT
    (1) the reduction of their level of economic interdependence with the industrialized countries.
    (2) the stabilization of world prices for their basic commodity exports.
    (3) increased control over monetary lending institutions such as the International Monetary Fund.
    (4) lower tariffs in industrialized countries for their exports.

	(1)*	(2)	(3)	(4)
Seniors	25.0	16.9	27.5	12.1
Freshmen	22.4	18.2	29.4	15.7
Two-Year	18.4	23.7	27.3	16.4

23. Between 1900 and 1979, numerous conferences and agreements intended to establish the conditions of international peace through prevention and control of war as well as through arms limitation fell short of their aims. Which of the following is LEAST important in explaining the lack of substantial progress toward world peace?
    (1) Sequences of arms buildup, followed by perceived threat, followed by another arms buildup by two rival nations or blocs of nations.
    (2) Failure to design and implement a system of collective security that nations can trust to preserve their safety and to protect their interests.
    (3) Destabilizing effects of war-related science and technology on arms limitation agreements.
    (4) The increase in the number of governments established by military coup and the number of governments currently dominated by military regimes.

	(1)	(2)	(3)	(4)*
Seniors	13.8	26.4	23.6	27.0
Freshmen	11.5	33.0	22.3	23.2
Two-Year	12.8	32.6	22.5	21.4

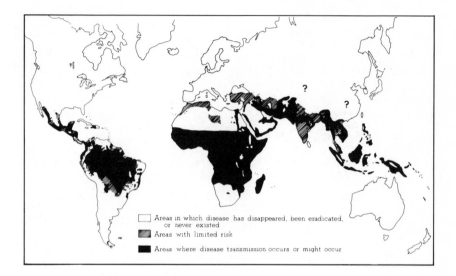

Areas in which disease has disappeared, been eradicated, or never existed

Areas with limited risk

Areas where disease transmission occurs or might occur

24. The map above shows the distribution in the world today of which of the following diseases?

(1) Bubonic plague
(2) Malaria
(3) Typhoid fever
(4) Cholera

	(1)	(2)*	(3)	(4)
Seniors	1.7	63.7	13.2	14.3
Freshmen	5.9	61.2	16.0	9.6
Two-Year	5.9	52.2	19.0	13.7

Who Are These Students?

The majority of the students in the survey are Democrats, tend toward the middle on a left/right political attitudes scale (although their parents, for the most part, lean toward the right), and come from parents of widely divergent educational backgrounds. Almost 15 percent of the seniors reported that their fathers had not finished high school, 25 percent of the two-year students said their mothers had not finished high school, but almost 20 percent of the seniors' fathers had professional or graduate degrees.

Although more than 95 percent of the entire sample reported that they were born in the United States, many of them did not seem certain just where that is. When asked to circle the region of the world where they were born, about 150 respondents circled Central America or South America. After some digging, the confused researchers discovered that those who had circled Central America had been born in the Midwest and those who had circled South America were from Tennessee, Virginia, and other southeastern states.

A greater proportion of this population reads daily newspapers than watches television, yet the main source of information about world affairs among all three groups is television. There were respondents who said they did not watch television, but most reported about 10 hours of viewing a week and some freshmen admitted to as much as 90 hours. Movies were the most popular TV fare among freshmen, news programs among seniors and two-year students. Most freshmen and seniors spent twice as many hours watching television as reading for pleasure.

In another question on the news media, students were asked to select four articles they would choose to read from a list of 16 fictitious headlines. In all three groups, the four international headlines in the list lost out to those announcing stories on the economy, medical technology, and science. The headlines and the percentage of seniors who chose each are shown in the accompanying box.

It was apparent from their responses to questions about their experiences in high school and college that the students believed they have had considerably more exposure to world problems and issues in high school classrooms than in col-

---

SENIORS' SELECTION OF NEWS ARTICLES
(*international articles)

53.1%	PRESIDENT CONSIDERING WAGE-PRICE FREEZE
49.5	TEAM OF NEW YORK SURGEONS RE-ATTACH MAN'S SEVERED LEG
46.7	ASTROPHYSICIST'S FINDINGS CAST LIGHT ON 'BLACK HOLES'
39.6	INDIAN GOVERNMENT STEPS UP VOLUNTARY STERILIZATION CAMPAIGN*
38.1	NEW COMPUTER TERMINAL 'TALKS' AND 'LISTENS'
28.6	SOVIET JEWS DENIED EXIT VISAS*
27.8	SALT II TALKS STALLED
21.7	MISSISSIPPI RIVER REACHES FLOOD STAGE
18.6	U.S. BALANCE OF PAYMENTS GLOOMY*
17.5	STEELERS FAVORED TO WIN SUPER BOWL
12.9	PRESIDENT THREATENS TO VETO APPROPRIATIONS BILL PASSED BY CONGRESS
11.7	SENATE COMMITTEE HEARS TESTIMONY ON CIVIL SERVICE REGULATIONS
10.3	U.S.-RUSSIAN WOMEN'S BASKETBALL PLAY-OFF EXPECTED IN OLYMPICS
9.9	REFEREE TURNS McENROE-NASTASE MATCH OVER TO UMPIRE
9.5	NEW LAND SPEED RECORD SET ON SALT FLATS
2.1	PROFESSIONAL SOCCER DRAWING RECORD CROWDS

---

lege. There are many plausible explanations for this response. High school classes are generally smaller, more open to discussion than college classes, and less restricted by disciplinary confines. Moreover, it is likely that more high school courses are taught from a current-events perspective.

History was chosen by most respondents as the subject (out of a list of 19) that had contributed to their awareness of world problems and issues. Foreign languages, although among the seven most frequently cited electives, were not highly rated as contributors to world understanding (see next section).

Average scores on the verbal section of the College Board's Scholastic Aptitude Test were 517 (freshmen), 547 (seniors), and 485 (two-year students); on the mathematical section, 536, 546, and 511. Average ACT (American College Testing Program) composite scores were 22, 23, and 19. The largest percentage of students in each group reported grade-point averages between 3.0 and 3.4.

How Students View the World

The problems of environmental pollution, denial of basic human rights, unemployment, intergroup conflict (apartheid, ethnic and religious persecution, etc.), depletion of natural resources, malnutrition and inadequate health care, inflation, and international conflict and war are, in the opinion of the three student groups, highly important, but some are more important than others. The students were asked to rate each of these world problems by assigning values to each of 11 scales such as *This problem is important, This problem is interesting to learn about*, or *This problem is solvable*. Values ranged from a low of 1 (*This problem is unimportant*) to a high of 5 (*This problem is important*). In the data on freshman responses, for example, international conflict and war had a mean (average) rating on the importance scale of 4.88, indicating that almost all (92.3 percent) of the freshmen thought it important.

The least important of these world problems, according to these freshmen, is intergroup conflict, which drew a rating of 3.75 and a ranking of eighth. Even this lowest rating, however, is still .75 above the midpoint which divides important from unimportant. These uniformly high ratings indicate that most if not all of these problems were considered highly important by these college students.

The respondents gave their highest ratings to the eight problems on these five scales:

- This problem is important;
- The American government can do a lot to solve this problem;
- This problem is related to many other problems;
- This problem is of concern to people in many parts of the world;
- This problem is long-term.

Thus the students saw these problems as important, interrelated, long-term, and of broad and universal concern. At the same time, they seemed to view these staggering problems as ones that could be solved by the American government.

In the survey of students' opinions, the three groups were asked to indicate the extent of their agreement (from 1 = strongly agree to 5 = strongly disagree) on the topics of chauvinism, world government, war, cooperation, and human rights. The seniors appeared to be the least indifferent to and most in disagreement with the chauvinist statements. For example, while a little more than a third (36.6) of the freshmen disagreed with the statement *The best way to insure peace is to keep the United States stronger than any other nation in the world*, almost half the seniors disagreed. *No duties are more important than duties toward one's country* provoked disagreement among more than half the seniors but only a third of the freshmen and two-year students. More interesting is the spread of responses: On even the most strongly worded statements, there is substantial agreement as well as disagreement. *No duties are more important than duties toward one's country* divided the freshmen almost evenly (39.8 percent agreed, 34.7 percent disagreed). Over a quarter of the freshmen and two-year students and a fifth of the seniors agreed with the statement *I'm for my country, right or wrong*.

Appreciable proportions of the three groups favor world government: About two-fifths believe that we should have a world government that could make binding laws, but two-thirds of the respondents in each group strongly disagreed that the United States should give up its independence to belong to such a government. Only about one in four students would prefer to be a citizen of the world than of a country.

The students were generally, but not unqualifiedly, opposed to war. The seniors in particular seemed reluctant to go along with some of the bolder generalizations such as *There is no conceivable justification for war*. More than half (52 percent) of that group disagreed with that statement. Similarly, more than one-third of the senior population agreed that *Under some conditions, war is necessary to maintain justice*.

Five questions on the Cooperation scale dealt with immigration of foreign peoples to the United States. The responses to these questions were characterized by contradictions in attitudes and an interesting balance of agreement and disagreement. Almost 20 percent more freshmen agreed than disagreed with the statement that *The immigration of foreigners to this country should be kept down so that we can provide for Americans first.* Yet almost half this group (44.3 percent) disagreed with the statement that *Immigrants should not be permitted to come into our country if they compete with our own workers.* On a third version of this question, the freshmen (as well as the other two groups) split their vote remarkably evenly:

25. The United States should be open to all those who wish to settle here.

	Strongly Agree	Agree	Indifferent	Disagree	Strongly Disagree
% Freshmen	7.4	31.4	22.4	32.1	6.7
% Seniors	7.7	32.1	21.3	34.6	4.4
% Two-Year	9.7	28.0	25.9	29.1	7.2

How Students View Themselves
The part of the survey devoted to students' perceptions of themselves consisted of 10 TRUE/FALSE statements designed to measure their interest in the world as well as their kinship with and concern for other people. For purposes of illustration, the statements have been grouped here according to these three categories.

Interest	*True*	*False*
1. I am interested in international relations and acquire information about international developments whenever I can.		
% Freshmen	60.3	39.7
% Seniors	65.3	34.7
% 2-Year	64.5	35.5
5. I rarely read news articles about international events.		
% Freshmen	26.0	74.0
% Seniors	20.3	79.7
% 2-Year	21.6	78.4

	True	False

8. I am not interested in studying other cultures.

	True	False
% Freshmen	12.1	87.9
% Seniors	12.1	87.9
% 2-Year	12.3	87.7

Kinship

3. I am most comfortable with people from my own culture.

	True	False
% Freshmen	78.6	21.4
% Seniors	77.9	22.1
% 2-Year	70.7	29.3

4. I feel a strong kinship with the world-wide human family.

	True	False
% Freshmen	41.4	58.6
% Seniors	42.4	57.6
% 2-Year	49.2	50.8

6. I find the customs of foreigners difficult to understand.

	True	False
% Freshmen	27.8	72.2
% Seniors	22.8	77.2
% 2-Year	28.7	71.3

9. I have almost nothing in common with people in underdeveloped nations.

	True	False
% Freshmen	28.0	72.0
% Seniors	27.7	72.3
% 2-Year	25.2	74.8

10. I make an effort to meet people from other countries.

	True	False
% Freshmen	60.0	40.0
% Seniors	58.6	41.4
% 2-Year	63.8	36.2

Concern

2. The fact that a flood can kill 25,000 people in India is very depressing to me.

	True	False
% Freshmen	70.5	29.5
% Seniors	69.0	31.0
% 2-Year	71.5	28.5

7. When I hear that thousands of people
    are starving in Cambodia, I feel very
    frustrated.

% Freshmen	69.4	30.6
% Seniors	71.6	28.4
% 2-Year	65.3	34.7

For every statement except number 8, there is a sizable percentage of students answering either TRUE or FALSE. This would seem to indicate that these students were not attempting to shape their answers to satisfy any particular ideal but were making a real effort to respond truthfully.

College Students and Foreign Languages
There seemed to be little interest in or enthusiasm for foreign languages among this group of students. Except for history, foreign language attracted the lowest percentage of freshmen as a possible major course of study. Most students in the survey felt that sociology, history, and economics had contributed more to their awareness of world problems than had foreign language study.

Ninety percent of the seniors and more than three-quarters of the other two groups had studied a foreign language, most having done so in the ninth and tenth grades, and slightly more than half the seniors had studied a foreign language in college. The most frequently reported foreign language studied by the students was Spanish, followed by French and German, in that order. About twice as many freshmen as seniors reported that they had studied English as a foreign language in elementary and secondary school. This might be a reflection of an increasing enrollment of foreign students at these levels or of the large proportion of two-year colleges located in border states.

The instruction these students received in foreign languages tended to emphasize a mastery of vocabulary and the rules of grammar rather than conversation skills.

More than half the students reported that they had been in a country other than the United States, most frequently on brief visits to Mexico or Canada. Very small numbers of respondents (less than 10 percent of any of the three groups) had participated in summer-abroad programs.

The final part of the language background section of the questionnaire consisted of three "can do" sets of self-assessment measures having to do with skills of speaking, listening, and reading. Each section consisted of a series of statements describing a language-use situation to which the respondent was required to indicate whether he or she could carry out that task "quite easily," "with some difficulty," or "with great difficulty or not at all." The situations described by the statements represented a wide range of proficiency, from the most basic survival types of language use to the kind of competency that might be expected of a native speaker.

Only about 60 percent of the students indicated that they can do even the simplest of speaking tasks "quite easily." Although almost half the seniors can introduce themselves in social situations and use appropriate greetings and leave-taking expressions, only about one-third can "give simple biographical information" about themselves (such as place of birth and schooling) and about one-tenth can talk about their favorite hobby with the same facility. The proportion of seniors who indicated that they can carry out particular language tasks "quite easily" is about the same as the proportion of freshmen.

The responses of the two-year students show a somewhat higher percentage of "quite easily" judgments, especially toward the end of the three sets of statements (for listening, speaking, and reading), where the tasks are more demanding. For example, on the speaking proficiency scale, 11.5 percent and 11.8 percent of the freshmen and seniors respectively indicated that they can talk about their favorite hobbies at some length using appropriate vocabulary; the corresponding figure for two-year students is 18 percent. Understanding a foreign movie without reading the subtitles is easy for 16 percent of the two-year students but only 9 percent of the freshmen and seniors. These differences may be attributable to the greater number of foreign students in the two-year group whose most proficient foreign language is English.

Although almost half the freshmen and seniors indicated that they are able to understand a native speaker who is speaking slowly and carefully, only 7 percent can easily understand one who is speaking at a normal conversational tempo. Reading comprehension showed a relatively low percentage of "quite easily" responses across all the "can do" statements. Almost half the seniors replied that they cannot easily read personal notes or letters written in simple words and constructions; more than half said that they cannot read newspaper headlines easily. Ninety percent feel that they cannot easily read a foreign newsmagazine without using a dictionary.

How Background, Experience, Attitudes, and Language Relate to Global Knowledge

How do these results of background, language, and attitudes correlate with performance on the knowledge test? How closely are students' backgrounds, language proficiency, and feelings about other peoples and cultures associated with their knowledge of the world about them?

Among the various *background* variables surveyed, only race and education of parents were significant. Both relate strongly to socioeconomic status, which in turn is closely associated with educational achievement. Not quite as strong but nevertheless significant was the correlation between the education of the students' parents and the way students in the three groups performed on the test. For example, the more education the parent(s) had had, the higher the scores their sons and daughters earned.

The highest *experience* correlations were found between scores on college admissions tests such as the College Board's Scholastic Aptitude Test (SAT) and the American College Testing Program (ACT) and performance on the knowledge tests. This is not surprising since scores on measures of academic aptitude such as the SAT often have a moderate to strong relationship to measures of achievement as also represented by this test. In fact, the relationship between admission test scores and the knowledge test is actually weaker than that between the SAT and College Board Achievement Tests in social studies, which suggests that there may be less of an aptitude factor in the knowledge test than had been expected. Grade-point average was also a significant correlate of global knowledge.

There is a clear relationship between students' methods of

acquiring information about the world and their scores on the knowledge test. Those students who reported that they are regular readers of international events in newspapers and other print media consistently scored higher on the test than those who acquire their information from television or radio news programs. Responses on the question that asked students to indicate headlines that interested them most were also highly correlated with the knowledge test. Those who chose headlines of international news stories ("Soviet Jews Denied Exit Visas," "U.S. Balance of Payments Gloomy," etc.) scored well on the knowledge test.

Among the *attitude* results, there was a high correlation between left political orientation and scores on the knowledge test. Those students scoring high on the test were in sympathy with the concerned, cooperative, pro-world government, pro-human rights, anti-war, and anti-chauvinistic sentiments measured by the survey's attitude scales.

The most surprising result of this analysis of correlations was the lack of relationship between *language* proficiency and world knowledge. The project staff discovered that while there is a definite relationship between knowledge and attitudes and between language and attitudes, there is no relationship between language and knowledge.

One hypothesis offered for this puzzling situation was a possible threshold level of language proficiency below which one does not have sufficient skill in the language to acquire information. Could it be that the students in the survey hadn't acquired enough skill in understanding and speaking foreign languages to make effective use of newspapers, magazines, and conversations with native speakers to acquire such knowledge?

The research staff pursued this question by separating the responses of the most highly proficient students (those who reported that they could "quite easily" carry out the five or seven most difficult "can do" tasks in the language questionnaire) from the others and analyzing their performance on the knowledge test. The results showed that the average scores earned by the most proficient students were not appreciably different from those earned by the total group. Thus the survey team had to conclude that there is essentially no relationship between proficiency in a modern foreign language and the overall level of global knowledge of U.S. college freshmen and seniors and two-year college students.

IV. Some Final Comments

The lack of knowledge of international affairs that is reflected in the low scores of all three groups of students would appear to be related to the general lack of interest in other nations and world issues among these students. More than a third of all three groups indicated on the attitude questionnaire that they were not interested in international relations. A fifth of the seniors and a quarter of the freshmen rarely read articles about international events. Less than 10 percent of these students have participated in exchange-student or summer-abroad programs at a time when such programs have increased dramatically.

An argument could be made that the students covered by the survey have a naive view of the world's problems. While most of them recognized that such problems as the denial of human rights, international conflict and war, and malnutrition and inadequate health care were indeed important and of universal concern, they also felt that they could be solved by the U.S. government. Moreover, the fact that the students rated malnutrition, intergroup (racial and religious) conflict, and denial of basic human rights consistently lowest on the "interest in," "know a lot about," and "important" scales suggests a limited, parochial view of the world.

The survey results showed clearly that students who are proficient in foreign languages are not necessarily informed about foreign affairs. There is a hint in these data, however, that those who are good at learning foreign languages have a greater interest in learning about international issues than those who are not. It may be that the interest was there but the opportunity was not, that foreign language instruction does not include effective experience with other cultures, as had been widely assumed.

The average senior in this sample of students is a woman, a B student who has studied Spanish for two years in high school and one year in college. She was taught by methods of language instruction that emphasized mastery of vocabulary and rules of grammar. Now, in her senior year, this student has forgotten a good deal of both the vocabulary and the grammar and has more difficulty than ever in speaking and understanding Spanish. It is not difficult to understand why this student was not interested in pursuing a foreign language as a major course of study.

It is not surprising that history majors were the highest scorers on the test, since many of the questions required some knowledge of history. What is discouraging is that history is the least popular major course of study among the freshmen in the sample. It would seem, then, that the study of history, which gives students a greater awareness of world issues than any other single subject field, is the least likely to be pursued by American college students.

Engineering and mathematics majors are involved with academic programs that have little to do with the content of the knowledge test. Yet these students scored almost as high on the test as the history majors. The test's emphasis on intellectual ability and the consistent finding that the more able students were generally the higher scorers may have been a contributing factor here. The most dismaying result was that education majors, the teachers of tomorrow, were the lowest scorers on the knowledge test.

Students are apparently acquiring information about international issues from the news media, but with mixed results. It is clear that students who read newspapers and newsmagazines know more about international issues than students who do not. However, students report that their main source of information about foreign affairs is television. But the ETS staff found no correlation between watching TV and global awareness.

Seniors averaged only about 8 points higher than freshmen on the knowledge test, a smaller difference than one would expect of students who have had four years of higher education. Perhaps such a result is to be expected, since there are not many opportunities to learn about foreign affairs on today's campuses. Global affairs is not a defined field of study in the college curriculum in the way that history or economics is and it is not, therefore, readily accessible to students in that form. As the students themselves reported in the survey, they spent more time discussing international issues in high school than in college. Thus, from this new evidence at hand, serious learning gaps at the college level would seem to persist even in 1980.

1981 Publications in the Education and the World View Series

The Role of the Scholarly Disciplines

This book focuses on the potential role of the disciplines in encouraging enlarged international dimensions in the undergraduate curriculum; it also provides useful insights into campus initiatives and effective curricular approaches.
$4.95

The World in the Curriculum: Curricular Strategies for the 21st Century

Written by Humphrey Tonkin of the University of Pennsylvania, this volume considers concrete, feasible recommendations for strengthening the international perspective of the undergraduate curriculum at academic institutions; it provides a guide to meaningful curricular change for top administrators and faculty.
$6.95

Education for a Global Century: Issues and Some Solutions

A reference handbook for faculty and administrators who wish to start or strengthen language and international programs, this contains descriptions of exemplary programs, definitions of minimal competencies in students' international awareness and knowledge, and recommendations of the project's national task force.
$7.95

Education and the World View

A book edition of Change's special issue on Education and the World View for use by trustees, faculty, and administrators; it also contains proceedings of a national conference that considered the implications of educational ethnocentrism and action to encourage change.
$6.95

What College Students Know About Their World

An important new national assessment of American freshmen and seniors, conducted by the Educational Testing Service, that covers the strengths and weaknesses of American college students' global understanding; an aid to faculty and program directors, it pinpoints areas for improving international content.
$5.95

ETS National Survey of Global Understanding

The full report of the 1980 national assessment of 3,000 college students about world cultures, foreign languages, and contemporary world issues. With complete data, charts, and analysis.
$10.95

Order from Change Magazine Press, 271 North Avenue, New Rochelle, N.Y. 10801. Add $1 if billing is desired.